Rewire:

Master Your Subconscious,
Release Your Suffering,
Create the Life You Deserve.

by

Trey Malicoat, M.S.

Copyright © 2023 by Trey Malicoat, M.S.

Rewire: Master your subconscious, Release your suffering, Create the life you deserve

Trey Malicoat, M.S.

First edition

All rights reserved. No part of this book may be reproduced or transmitted in any form or by any means, electronic or mechanical, including photocopying, recording, or by any information storage and retrieval system, without permission in writing from the copyright holder.

Published 2023 by Restoration Academy Press, Denver, Colorado

ISBN 979-8-9892079-1-6

Library of Congress Cataloging-in-Publication Data is available.

For presentations, consultations, or coaching services, please get in touch with Trey directly at www.treymalicoat.com

To learn more about our other classes, retreats, support groups, or the Restoration Model for Emotional Healing, please visit www.restorationcoaches.com.

Please note that the information presented in this book is solely for general enjoyment and should not be considered advice. Please consult a professional with emotional, social, legal, physical, or other needs.

Dedication

I want to personally thank every client who has informed my understanding of human behavior and the power of the subconscious. Thank you for journeying with me to discover how to live peacefully, presently, and with abundant love.

In Gratitude,

Getting the Most from This Book

I invite you to journal and reflect on your personal experiences as you read this book. Journaling is a powerful tool for self-reflection and growth. It can help you to:

- Gain clarity and understanding about your thoughts, feelings, and experiences.
- Identify patterns and themes in your life.
- Develop insights into your motivations and behaviors.
- Set goals and make plans for your future.
- Process difficult emotions and experiences.
- Connect with your inner wisdom and intuition.

Here are some tips for journaling:

- Find a quiet, comfortable space where you won't be interrupted.
- Set aside regular time to journal, even if it's just for a few minutes each day.
- Start by reviewing the information and prompts in the book. Then, write freely and honestly without judgment. Your journal is a safe space.
- Be specific and concrete in your writing.
- Describe your thoughts, feelings, and experiences in detail.
- Don't be afraid to explore difficult emotions and experiences.
- Revisit your journal entries regularly to track your progress and growth.
- Consider pairing journaling with a creative activity, such as drawing, painting, or music. This can help you to express yourself more deeply.

Journaling is a journey, not a destination. There is no right or wrong way to journal. The most important thing is to be consistent and to find a method that works for you.

Here are some additional tips that I have learned from my own experience:

- Be patient with yourself. It takes time to develop a journaling practice. Don't get discouraged if you don't feel like you're "doing it right" at first. Just keep writing, and you will eventually find your way.
- Experiment with different types of journaling. There are many ways to journal, so find a method that works for you. You can write in a traditional journal or try freewriting, stream-of-consciousness journaling, or gratitude journaling.
- Don't be afraid to be creative. Journaling is a wonderful way to express yourself creatively. You can express your thoughts and feelings through art, music, or poetry.
- Share your journal with others. If you feel comfortable, you can share your journal with a therapist, friend, or family member. This can help you to get feedback and support on your journey.

I hope these tips help you to get started with journaling. Journaling has been personally transformative. I hope you have a similar experience.

"To explore the depths of your mind is to embark on a lifelong adventure, where the subconscious holds the map to your true self."

TABLE OF CONTENTS

Introduction 1
Chapter 1 - Unveiling the Subconscious Mind's Mysteries 4
Chapter 2 - The Driving Forces: Pursuit of Pleasure and Mitigation of Fear 7
Chapter 3 - Our Natural State: Equilibrium, Safety, and Functionality 10
Chapter 4 - The Invisible Threads That Shape Us 14
Chapter 5 - Analyzing the Subconscious Mind: Unveiling the Hidden Layers 18
Chapter 6 - The Inner Workings of Transformation 23
Chapter 7 - The Restoration Model for Emotional Healing 27
Chapter 8 - Practical Strategies for Transformation 32
Chapter 9 - Navigating Challenges on the Path of Transformation 36
Chapter 10 - Embracing the Journey: Celebrating Growth and Healing 40
Chapter 11 - Sharing Your Journey and Inspiring Others 44
Chapter 12 - Sustaining Your Transformation 48
Chapter 13 - Cultivating an Abundant Life 52
Chapter 14 - The Ever-Unfolding Journey 57
Conclusion - Embracing the Subconscious Journey to Intentional Living 61
Chapter Summaries 65
Journaling Guide 70
Prompts for Exploring Your Subconscious Mind 80
References 87
Index 89
About The Author 99

Introduction

Hello there, I'm Trey Malicoat. Join me on an exciting journey into the fascinating realm of your subconscious mind. This silent realm holds incredible power to shape your thoughts, feelings, and behaviors.

As a coach, therapist, and founder of the Restoration Model for Emotional Healing, I've witnessed people transform their lives by tapping into the potential of their subconscious minds. In this book, I'll guide you on this voyage of self-discovery and personal growth.

The idea of the subconscious mind may sound mysterious, but don't worry - we'll explore it in simple terms. Picture your mind as an iceberg, with the tip above water representing your conscious thoughts. Below the surface lies your subconscious, influencing over 90% of your mental activity.

Think of the subconscious as a "silent partner" in your life, continually shaping your choices, relationships, and health. It's like having a hidden crew backstage, directing the play of your thoughts and actions.

In the following pages, we'll dive into how your subconscious mind developed, its vital roles, and its incredible potential for positive change. We'll examine the primal motivations driving human behavior - seeking pleasure and avoiding fear.

My work involves thoroughly analyzing individuals - their histories, influences, suffering, and patterns - to gain profound insights into their subconscious worlds. This understanding provides the foundation to create empowering new belief systems and take control of your life in the present moment.

I'll introduce techniques like core belief restructuring, affirmations, visualization, CBT, hypnotherapy, and more - designed to reshape your subconscious mind and guide you toward transformation.

Finally, we'll explore the Restoration Model for Emotional Healing, a powerful approach for living consciously and creatively, with intention in your relationships. You can unlock your true potential by objectively assessing yourself in the now, interrupting unhelpful patterns, and seizing control of your life with purpose.

This book is your roadmap to unveil the hidden power within. It's a journey of self-discovery, growth, and transformation. Join me as we embark on this incredible adventure into the world of your subconscious mind, and together, we'll uncover the keys to a fulfilling, intentional life.

"Your subconscious is the source of your intuition, creativity, and inner wisdom. Dive deep and harness its power."

Chapter 1

Unveiling the Subconscious Mind's Mysteries

Welcome to the fascinating realm of the human psyche, where mysteries abound, and the subconscious plays a leading role. In this chapter, we'll embark on a journey to understand the profound influence of your hidden subconscious mind.

Imagine your conscious mind as the calm surface of a serene lake, thoughts drifting by like gentle ripples. Beneath lies a complex hidden world - your subconscious mind. Like a vast underground library, it contains over 90% of your mental activity, working tirelessly behind the scenes.

We often call the subconscious the "silent partner" in life because it continually shapes your thoughts, emotions, and actions, even when you're unaware. From the moment you're born, your subconscious mind begins forming, influenced by the people and experiences around you.

Early in life, your parents, teachers, and other significant figures become the architects of your subconscious. They impart beliefs, values, and rules integral to your subconscious programming - the foundation for your thoughts, emotions, and behaviors.

The subconscious mind serves several vital functions:

1. Storing Memories: Your subconscious is an infinite vault containing vast amounts of information, including memories you

may not consciously recall. These memories shape your perceptions and reactions.
2. Regulating Emotions: Ever wonder why you react in specific ways to situations? Your subconscious manages your emotions, filtering how you experience and express feelings.
3. Making Decisions: While conscious thought drives decisions, your subconscious is always at work - guiding every step you take, assessing speed, and avoiding obstacles.
4. Learning New Skills: Whenever you acquire a new skill, like riding a bike or typing, your subconscious tirelessly rehearses the information until it becomes second nature.

Your subconscious also dramatically influences your choices, relationships, and well-being. It's the unseen force that drives you to gravitate toward certain people, make decisions, or respond to life's challenges in particular ways.

Psychology, neuroscience, philosophy, and religion offer distinct perspectives on the subconscious mind. Psychologists contend it's the power behind thoughts, feelings, and behaviors and can be reshaped through therapy and techniques. Neuroscientists study the brain's intricacies, showing the subconscious plays essential roles in memory, emotion, and decision-making.

Philosophically, the subconscious mind has been argued to shape our understanding of reality and self. Many religious beliefs hold that the subconscious is a gateway to spiritual experiences, enabling connections with higher selves and enlightenment.

Understanding your subconscious mind is like discovering a hidden treasure within yourself. You can learn to harness its power by unraveling its secrets and creating positive change. So, stay with me on this journey as we dive deeper into the mysteries of your subconscious and unlock your inner potential.

"Exploring the subconscious is like diving into a well of infinite wisdom. Drink deeply from its waters."

Chapter 2

The Driving Forces: Pursuit of Pleasure and Mitigation of Fear

Welcome back! In our journey through the fascinating subconscious mind, we've arrived at a crucial crossroads - the two fundamental driving forces behind human behavior: the relentless pursuit of pleasure and the unwavering determination to mitigate fear.

The Pursuit of Pleasure:

One primary motivator of human behavior is the pursuit of pleasure. Think of it as a magnetic force pulling you toward experiences that bring joy, satisfaction, and fulfillment. This pursuit is deeply ingrained in your subconscious, driving you to seek pleasurable experiences and avoid pain.

From savoring a delicious meal to achieving a meaningful goal, pursuing pleasure is a constant companion. You're wired to seek pleasurable experiences because they provide a sense of reward and well-being.

For example, when you bite into a favorite dessert, your subconscious releases feel-good chemicals like dopamine, creating pleasure and reward. These experiences reinforce your desire to seek similar pleasures again.

Mitigation of Fear:

On the flip side, we're equally motivated by mitigating fear. Fear is primal - it has evolved to keep us safe from harm. Your subconscious mind is designed to detect threats and activate your fight-or-flight response for protection.

Imagine encountering a wild animal in the woods. Your subconscious springs into action, flooding your body with adrenaline and sharpening your focus for survival. This is your subconscious at work, prioritizing your safety.

However, fear isn't limited to physical threats - it extends to emotional and psychological aspects of life. We fear rejection, failure, uncertainty, and more. These perceived dangers can be just as potent, with your subconscious tirelessly working to protect you.

The Interplay of Pleasure and Fear:

What makes these driving forces even more intriguing is how they interact. Pleasure and fear often dance together in our subconscious minds, shaping decisions and emotions. For example, the fear of missing out can compel us to seek pleasure in social situations, while the fear of failure may hold us back from pursuing dreams.

Understanding this interplay is crucial, shedding light on why we make certain choices and how we can navigate the landscape of desires and fears. By acknowledging these forces and learning to manage them, we gain greater control over our lives and make more intentional decisions.

In the chapters ahead, we'll delve even deeper into how pleasure and fear shape thoughts, emotions, and actions. We'll explore real-life examples, insights, and practical strategies to help harness these forces for growth and transformation.

So, as we continue our journey, remember that the pursuit of pleasure and mitigation of fear are loyal companions on the path of life. Understanding their roles in your subconscious mind will give you valuable insights to lead a more fulfilling, intentional life.

"In the silence of your subconscious, you'll hear the whispers of your inner truth."

– Trey Malicoat.

Chapter 3

Our Natural State: Equilibrium, Safety, and Functionality

Welcome back to our exploration of the subconscious mind. In previous chapters, we've unraveled the mysteries behind this hidden powerhouse and the driving forces of pleasure and fear. Now, let's dive into our natural state - characterized by equilibrium, safety, and functionality.

Envision your subconscious mind as a delicate balancing act, seeking harmony in the ever-changing landscape of thoughts and emotions.

Equilibrium:

Imagine standing on a tightrope, perfectly balanced between two worlds. This represents equilibrium - a state where opposing forces are in harmony. In your subconscious mind, equilibrium is critical to emotional stability and well-being.

When thoughts, emotions, and actions are in equilibrium, you feel centered and grounded, better equipped to manage challenges and navigate life's twists and turns. It's like having a solid foundation to build your life.

Consider the opposite - when equilibrium is disrupted, leading to emotional turmoil, stress, and uncertainty. Restoring balance when disrupted is a driving force behind many subconscious decisions and behaviors. We instinctively seek to regain equilibrium when it's disturbed.

Safety:

Now, let's discuss safety - a fundamental human need. Your subconscious mind is like a vigilant guardian, constantly assessing your environment for threats and your level of safety.

You learned to distinguish between safe and unsafe situations from an early age. Your subconscious internalizes these lessons, shaping beliefs and behaviors. For example, if you grew up in a nurturing environment, your subconscious views the world as safe. If you face adversity or trauma, your subconscious may see the world as more dangerous.

Feeling safe is essential for overall well-being, allowing you to trust others and explore opportunities. Conversely, a constant sense of danger can lead to anxiety, hypervigilance, and reluctance to take risks.

Functionality:

Imagine a well-oiled machine operating smoothly - that's functionality. In your natural state, you experience functionality as the ability to navigate life's challenges confidently and competently.

Functionality encompasses your capacity to adapt, learn, and grow. It's the sense you can handle whatever life brings. Your subconscious plays a huge role in maintaining this state of functionality.

However, functionality is dynamic, not static. Life brings constant change, and your subconscious must continuously adapt to new circumstances and challenges. This adaptability is crucial for maintaining equilibrium and safety.

Influences on Our Natural State:

As we delve deeper into the subconscious mind, we must recognize factors influencing our natural state:

1. Parental Programming: Our parents and caregivers pass down beliefs and values that shape our perception of equilibrium, safety, and functionality.

2. Personal Experiences: Experiences of suffering, trauma, loss, and transition can disrupt our sense of equilibrium and safety, leaving subconscious imprints influencing beliefs and behaviors.
3. Individual Factors: Our unique physiology, neurochemistry, and genetics significantly influence how we perceive and respond to the world, determining our natural state.

Recognizing these influences is vital to better understanding ourselves. By examining how our beliefs about safety and functionality formed, we gain valuable insights into our thoughts, emotions, and actions.

In the chapters ahead, we'll explore how these influences manifest in life and how to achieve a more balanced, safe, and functional existence. Your subconscious mind is your ally on this journey, and by unlocking its potential, you can work toward equilibrium, safety, and functionality to thrive in life's ever-changing landscape.

"In the labyrinth of your subconscious, you'll discover the threads that weave the tapestry of your existence."

Chapter 4

The Invisible Threads That Shape Us

Welcome back to our expedition through the hidden depths of the subconscious mind. In previous chapters, we've unraveled the mysteries of our natural state - equilibrium, safety, and functionality. Let's delve into the invisible threads shaping our beliefs, thoughts, and behaviors.

Imagine these threads as the intricate tapestry of your subconscious mind, woven from your personal history, family indoctrination, and life's many experiences.

Personal History:

Your personal history is like a storybook capturing the events, encounters, and milestones shaping your life. These experiences are the threads weaving the fabric of your subconscious mind.

Consider your earliest memories, triumphs and challenges faced in school, and significant moments leaving a lasting impact. Each experience contributed to forming your beliefs, values, and self-perception.

For example, you likely developed strong self-worth and confidence if you received praise and encouragement for achievements as a child. Conversely, if you faced criticism for poor performance, it may have led to self-doubt or limiting beliefs.

Family Indoctrination:

Family is a powerful force in shaping our subconscious minds. From an early age, we absorb our parents' and caregivers' beliefs and values. These teachings become integral to our subconscious programming.

Consider the values your family instilled in you - the importance of hard work, honesty, or loyalty. These often form the bedrock of your belief system, influencing decisions and actions.

However, family indoctrination isn't limited to positive values. It can also pass down fears, prejudices, and limiting beliefs. If your parents held deep-seated financial worries, you may have absorbed those, impacting your relationship with money as an adult.

Life's Experiences:

Life is an evolving journey filled with experiences molding our subconscious minds. Whether love, loss, or overcoming obstacles, each experience leaves an imprint.

Particularly influential are experiences of suffering, trauma, powerlessness, and transition. These moments can shake our equilibrium and safety, leaving emotional scars and ingrained beliefs.

For instance, trauma can lead your subconscious to develop defense mechanisms to avoid reliving that trauma. These mechanisms affect your thoughts, emotions, and behaviors, sometimes without conscious awareness.

The Cumulative Effect:

It's essential to understand these influences don't operate in isolation. Instead, they accumulate and intertwine, creating a complex web guiding your life.

Your personal history, family indoctrination, and life experiences come together to form the lens through which you view the world. This lens shapes your perceptions, reactions, and decisions, often subconsciously.

Recognizing the invisible threads shaping you is pivotal for self-awareness and growth. Examining these influences gives you insight into the core beliefs driving your thoughts and behaviors. You can start to unravel limiting beliefs and replace them with empowering ones.

In the chapters ahead, we'll explore how to navigate these invisible threads, understand their impact, and begin reshaping your subconscious mind. Remember, you can reweave the tapestry of your beliefs and thoughts, creating a more intentional and fulfilling life.

"Unlocking the potential of your subconscious is the key to unlocking the potential of your life."

Chapter 5

Analyzing the Subconscious Mind: Unveiling the Hidden Layers

Welcome back to our exploration of the intricate workings of the subconscious mind. In previous chapters, we've peeled back layers to reveal how personal history, family indoctrination, and life experiences shape beliefs and thoughts. Now, we'll embark on a deeper analysis of the subconscious mind's hidden layers.

Envision your subconscious as a vast, multidimensional puzzle waiting to be solved.

Controlling Behaviors:

One of the first layers we encounter is controlling behaviors - automatic responses and habits arising without conscious thought. They often serve as coping mechanisms or ways to maintain control.

For example, trauma can lead to controlling behaviors that create predictability and order. These behaviors may manifest as an intense need for structure or fear of uncertainty.

Irrational Beliefs:

Beneath the surface, irrational beliefs lurk in the subconscious depths. These ingrained beliefs can distort the perception of reality, leading to self-doubt, negative self-talk, or unrealistic expectations.

For instance, holding an irrational belief that you must be perfect can trigger feelings of inadequacy and anxiety when you make mistakes. Like invisible chains, these beliefs hold you back from your full potential.

Defense Mechanisms:

Delving deeper, we encounter defense mechanisms - strategies your mind employs to protect from discomfort or pain. While once useful, they can limit growth and self-awareness.

Common defense mechanisms include denial, projection, and repression. For example, unresolved grief may lead you to deny painful emotions through avoidance. These mechanisms can keep you trapped in cycles of avoidance and emotional numbness.

Attachment Styles:

Our attachment styles, formed early through caregiver interactions, play a significant subconscious role - influencing how we create and maintain relationships throughout life.

There are four primary styles: secure, anxious, avoidant, and disorganized. Each impacts beliefs about relationships, intimacy, and trust. Understanding your style sheds light on patterns and helps you navigate them effectively.

Developmental Staging of the Person:

Continuing our descent, we encounter the developmental staging of the person. This explores how psychological and emotional development unfolds through life stages.

For example, adolescence often involves grappling with identity, autonomy, self-worth, and the desire for approval. Understanding your stage provides insights into current challenges and growth opportunities.

Current and Past Coping Skills:

Coping skills are tools in your subconscious toolbox for navigating challenges. Some are adaptive, helping you thrive in adversity. Others may be maladaptive, hindering progress.

For example, suppressing emotions as a coping mechanism can impact expressing yourself and connecting with others. Recognizing coping skills, helpful and unhelpful, is crucial for emotional growth.

Indications or History of Psychopathology:

Deeper still, we may uncover indications of mental health challenges shaping your subconscious mind - anxiety, depression, PTSD, or others. These can profoundly influence thoughts, emotions, and behaviors.

Understanding your mental health history allows you to seek appropriate support and strategies to manage these challenges - a vital step toward emotional healing and growth.

Emotional and Intellectual Functioning:

Your emotional and intellectual functioning drives your thoughts and behaviors. Emotional intelligence, self-awareness, and critical thinking all play roles in navigating life's complexities.

Examining these capabilities provides a clearer understanding of your strengths and growth areas.

Rigid Thought and Belief Patterns:

At the deepest layer, we may uncover rigid thought and belief patterns deeply entrenched in our subconscious mind. These resistant patterns often underlie persistent life challenges.

For instance, rigidly believing vulnerability is a weakness can hinder authentic connections with others. Identifying and challenging these patterns is transformative, enabling growth and change.

Maladaptive Relational Patterns:

Finally, we encounter maladaptive relational patterns governing interactions with others, leading to recurring relationship issues.

For example, avoiding conflict can hinder communication and problem-solving. Recognizing and changing these patterns fosters healthier, more fulfilling connections.

Analyzing these hidden layers provides profound insights into the beliefs, thoughts, and behaviors shaping your life. In the chapters ahead, we'll explore transforming these layers, helping you unravel the mysteries of your mind and embark on profound personal growth and emotional healing.

"Your subconscious is the bridge between your past and your future. Cross it with purpose."

CHAPTER 6

THE INNER WORKINGS OF TRANSFORMATION

Welcome back to our expedition through the subconscious mind's hidden depths. Previously, we've peeled back layers revealing irrational beliefs, defense mechanisms, and more. Now, we'll dive into the inner workings of transformation.

Core Belief Restructuring:

Central to transformation is core belief restructuring. Envision your core beliefs as a house's foundation - you build everything upon them. Often developing early in life, these beliefs can be deeply ingrained in your subconscious mind.

Restructuring involves comprehensively understanding your core beliefs - their origins, function, and alignment with current values and goals. This creates cognitive dissonance - discomfort motivating change.

For example, believing you're unworthy of love, you can explore its origins, challenge its validity, and replace it with self-love and self-acceptance. Like renovating your mind's foundation, this process paves the way for new possibilities.

Positive Affirmations:

Positive affirmations powerfully reshape subconscious beliefs. They are concise, uplifting statements you repeat regularly, reprogramming your subconscious with positive beliefs.

If you struggle with self-confidence, repeating affirmations like "I am worthy and capable" boosts confidence by replacing negative self-talk and limiting beliefs. Consistency helps affirmations become internalized, influencing thoughts, feelings, and behaviors.

Visualization:

Visualization involves creating vivid mental images of desired outcomes. Visualizing success, happiness, or achievement makes your subconscious believe these outcomes are possible.

It engages your subconscious power to manifest your visions into reality by providing a roadmap to follow.

Cognitive Behavioral Therapy (CBT):

Cognitive Behavioral Therapy (CBT) identifies and changes negative thought patterns. By challenging and reframing distorted thoughts, individuals can transform behaviors and emotions.

CBT is invaluable for reshaping the subconscious mind over time. It helps recognize automatic negative thoughts, examine their validity, and replace them with more constructive beliefs.

Hypnotherapy:

Hypnotherapy induces deep relaxation where the subconscious becomes highly receptive to suggestion. A trained therapist guides you to access and reprogram subconscious beliefs in this state.

During hypnotherapy, you can explore and reframe limiting beliefs, release emotional blockages, and implant positive suggestions deep within your subconscious - a powerful catalyst for change.

Neuro-Linguistic Programming (NLP):

Neuro-Linguistic Programming (NLP) uses language patterns to change thoughts, feelings, and behaviors. It involves understanding the thought and language patterns governing your subconscious mind.

NLP techniques help identify and change unhelpful language patterns, reframe negative self-talk, and cultivate more empowering beliefs and behaviors.

Meditation:

Meditation helps focus attention and quiet the mind. It allows greater awareness of subconscious thoughts and beliefs by non-judgmentally observing passing thoughts.

This self-awareness is crucial for transformation, enabling recognition and change of unhelpful beliefs.

Exposure Therapy:

Exposure therapy helps individuals confront and overcome fears and anxiety by gradually exposing themselves to fearful thoughts or situations in a controlled, safe environment.

For instance, if you fear public speaking, exposure therapy progressively faces you with speaking situations. Over time, your subconscious learns these situations aren't as threatening as perceived.

Creative Visioning:

Creative visioning explores desires for your ideal life. It taps into subconscious creativity and intuition to set meaningful goals.

Aligning conscious desires with subconscious aspirations creates powerful synergy, propelling you toward your dreams.

The Restoration Model integrates these methods to help individuals live consciously, intentionally, and creatively. By objectively assessing yourself, interrupting maladaptive patterns, and taking purposeful control of life, you can unlock your true potential and experience profound personal growth.

In the chapters ahead, we'll explore these transformational methods further, providing practical tools to harness your subconscious power and create an intentional, purpose-driven life.

"The most profound insights often emerge from the silent whispers of your subconscious mind."

Chapter 7

The Restoration Model for Emotional Healing

Welcome back to our journey through the intricate subconscious mind. Previously, we've explored various transformational tools and techniques. Now, we'll delve into the comprehensive Restoration Model for Emotional Healing.

Let's explore the principles and practices underpinning this holistic model for transforming the subconscious mind and facilitating emotional healing. As you explore each principle, please consider how to make them a daily practice for ongoing emotional mastery. Doing so will force you to step out of limiting and painful stories and create a life of joy, peace, and purpose.

Living in the Present:

The first pillar of the Restoration Model is living in the present. Your subconscious mind dwells on the past and future - unresolved emotions and unfinished business.

Living in the present means shifting awareness to the here and now, embracing the present moment with its challenges and beauty. This creates a sense of grounded presence, allowing you to engage with life as it unfolds fully.

Intentional Living:

Intentional living is the second pillar. It emphasizes the power of conscious choice to shape your life instead of being driven by automatic thoughts and behaviors.

When you live intentionally, you set clear goals and align actions with your values, making choices reflecting your deepest desires and aspirations. Your subconscious becomes a willing partner in manifesting your intentions.

Creative Expression:

The third pillar is creative expression. Your subconscious is a wellspring of creativity, often untapped. Creative expression allows you to access and channel this hidden creativity.

Engaging in creative activities fosters a deep connection with your subconscious. It enables you to explore your inner world, unearth buried emotions, and bring them to the surface for healing and transformation.

Personal Empowerment:

Personal empowerment forms the fourth pillar. It's about taking control of life by standing in your power. Instead of being a passive passenger, you become the driver of your destiny.

Empowerment means recognizing your inner strength, resilience, and capacity for change. It's shedding limitations imposed by subconscious beliefs and stepping into your potential.

Love in Relationship:

The fifth pillar focuses on love in relationships. The subconscious mind profoundly influences human connections. By fostering love, empathy, and understanding in relationships, you create an environment for healing and growth.

This pillar emphasizes nurturing healthy relationships and self-love. Self-compassion is essential for emotional healing. Treat yourself with the same kindness you offer others.

With Self-Understanding:

The Restoration Model strongly emphasizes self-understanding. Gaining insight into the drivers of your subconscious mind unlocks the power to transform them.

Objectively assessing yourself in the present is the first step - thoroughly examining your beliefs, behaviors, and emotional responses. This self-awareness is the foundation upon which all other pillars are built.

Interrupting Maladaptive Patterns:

The next step is interrupting maladaptive patterns. Your subconscious may have developed unhelpful coping and defense mechanisms.

You can interrupt their automatic activation by recognizing these patterns and understanding their origins. This allows replacing them with more constructive responses.

Taking Control of Your Life:

The Restoration Model empowers you to take control of life by standing in your power. This means making choices aligned with your values, desires, and intentions, setting clear goals, and taking deliberate action.

As you reclaim control, you begin steering your life intentionally rather than being influenced by subconscious forces.

Creating with Purpose:

The Restoration Model encourages purposeful creation. You become a co-creator of your reality by aligning conscious intentions with subconscious beliefs.

This creative process involves setting meaningful goals, using visualization techniques, and tapping your innate creativity to design your desired life.

The Restoration Model provides a comprehensive framework for understanding and transforming the subconscious mind. It combines self-awareness, intentionality, creative expression, empowerment, and nurturing relationships to facilitate deep emotional healing and personal growth.

In the chapters ahead, we'll explore practical strategies based on this model, providing the tools and guidance needed to embark on a transformative journey of self-discovery, healing, and intentional living.

"Your subconscious is a vast universe waiting to be explored. The deeper you go, the more wonders you'll find."

Chapter 8

Practical Strategies for Transformation

Welcome back to our exploration of the Restoration Model. Previously, we've delved into its principles and pillars. Now, let's dive into practical strategies to put these into action.

Let's explore techniques designed to empower emotional healing and growth.

Daily Mindfulness Practice:

A powerful tool for living presently and fostering self-awareness is mindfulness. Daily practice involves setting aside time to focus on the present moment non-judgmentally.

Start with short sessions, gradually increasing the duration as you become more comfortable. Pay attention to thoughts, emotions, and bodily sensations. This heightened awareness helps understand subconscious patterns.

Journaling for Self-Reflection:

Journaling promotes self-reflection. Dedicate a few minutes daily to write down thoughts, feelings, and experiences. Use it to explore beliefs, challenges, and aspirations.

Also, track your progress - record growth insights, achievements, and positive affirmations to integrate into daily life.

Affirmation Practice:

Positive affirmations are invaluable for reshaping beliefs. Create a list reflecting your intentions for growth and healing. These should be concise, positive, and present-focused.

If working on self-confidence, an affirmation could be: "I am confident and capable in all I do." Repeat these regularly, aloud, or silently. Consistency helps replace negative self-talk and limiting beliefs.

Visualization Techniques:

Visualization harnesses your subconscious creativity. Set aside time to imagine desired outcomes in detail and with emotion vividly.

Visualize yourself succeeding, feeling confident, and achieving goals. This powerfully signals your subconscious to align with your conscious intentions.

Cognitive Restructuring:

Cognitive restructuring identifies and challenges negative thought patterns. When unhelpful, limiting thoughts arise, examine their validity.

Ask yourself, "Is this thought evidence-based?" or "Is there a more rational perspective?" Reframing thoughts can reprogram beliefs over time.

Creative Expression:

Engage in creative activities to tap into subconscious creativity and emotions. Let thoughts and feelings flow freely through art, music, writing, or other forms.

Creativity can be cathartic, helping access and release buried emotions. It also promotes self-awareness and personal growth.

Setting Clear Intentions:

Intentional living starts with clear life intentions. Write down short and long-term personal and professional goals. Clarify values and your desired life.

A clear sense of purpose and direction aligns your subconscious with conscious intentions. Your beliefs and behaviors naturally fall into place.

Nurturing Relationships:

Actively nurture healthy connections. Practice empathy, listening, and open communication. Share thoughts and feelings with trusted friends or a therapist.

Also, remember to extend self-love and compassion. Self-care is fundamental for resilience as you navigate challenges.

Embracing Personal Empowerment:

Empowerment means recognizing inner strength and resilience. Create a list of strengths, accomplishments, and moments of growth.

Reflect on your capacity for change and transformation. Celebrate achievements, no matter how small. Embracing empowerment breaks limiting beliefs and patterns.

These practical strategies provide a roadmap for the Restoration Model's principles in daily life. Incorporating them unlocks your subconscious potential, guiding you on a transformative journey of self-discovery, healing, and intentional living.

"Knowing your conscious self is wisdom, but knowing your subconscious self is enlightenment."

Chapter 9

Navigating Challenges on the Path of Transformation

Welcome back to our exploration of the Restoration Model. We've delved into principles, practices, and strategies. Now, let's address the inevitable challenges arising on this path of self-discovery and growth.

Resistance to Change:

A primary challenge is resistance to change. Your subconscious mind is accustomed to existing beliefs and patterns, even if unhelpful. Attempting to replace them with new, empowering ones can elicit resistance.

Resistance often manifests as self-doubt, fear, or discomfort. It's important to acknowledge this is natural in the process - a sign your subconscious mind is grappling with change. Rather than succumbing, use it as a catalyst for growth. Reaffirm your commitment to goals and remind yourself of the benefits of change.

Impatience and Frustration:

Transformation unfolds over time, and impatience and frustration often arise. You may want immediate results, but the subconscious typically changes gradually.

To overcome impatience, set realistic expectations for your progress. Celebrate small victories, recognizing every step forward brings you closer to your goals. Patience and persistence are allies on this journey.

Self-Doubt and Negative Self-Talk:

Negative self-talk and self-doubt can persistently challenge transformation. Your subconscious mind may undermine confidence with past limiting beliefs.

Counteract negative thoughts using positive affirmations and cognitive restructuring. Remind yourself of your strengths and achievements. Seek support from friends, a therapist, or a mentor for encouragement and perspective.

Relapse and Setbacks:

It's essential to acknowledge relapse, and setbacks are part of the process. You may revert to old behaviors and thought patterns after making progress. This is normal, not failure.

Rather than viewing setbacks as defeats, consider them opportunities for learning and growth. Analyze triggers and identify strategies to prevent them in the future. Remember that transformation is an ongoing journey of ups and downs.

Overcoming Comfort Zones:

Transformation often requires stepping outside comfort zones. Your subconscious mind may resist change, perceiving the familiar as safe, even if not ideal.

Challenge yourself to embrace discomfort as a sign of growth. Be open to new experiences and pushing boundaries. Gradually, your subconscious adjusts to expanded comfort zones.

Dealing with Emotional Residue:

Exploring your subconscious may surface buried emotions and unresolved issues - challenging to process. Seeking a coach or therapist's guidance and support can be immensely helpful to navigate and release them safely.

They can provide validation, techniques, and a supportive environment to process emotional residue healthily.

Balancing Self-Care:

Transformation can be demanding, making self-care crucial for maintaining well-being. Prioritize exercise, meditation, nutrition, rest, and other practices in your routine.

Self-care provides resilience and adaptability to navigate challenges on your journey.

Staying Committed to Intentions:

Life's demands and distractions can divert focus from intentions and goals. Regularly revisiting your intentions reinforces commitment. Surround yourself with visual reminders and nurture a support system to encourage your journey.

Embracing Uncertainty:

Transformation often involves uncertainty. Your subconscious mind may resist, craving predictability and stability. Practice mindfulness to stay present in uncertainty. Remind yourself that change leads to growth and opportunities. Embrace the unknown as a gateway to transformation.

Navigating these challenges requires patience, self-compassion, and resilience. Remember, the journey holds value, with each challenge presenting opportunities for growth and self-discovery. With determination and commitment to your intentions, you can overcome obstacles and continue your transformative journey toward emotional healing and intentional living.

"Celebrate your growth, heal your wounds, and continue blossoming into your highest potential."

Chapter 10

Embracing the Journey: Celebrating Growth and Healing

Welcome back to our exploration of the Restoration Model. We've delved into principles, practices, strategies, and challenges. Let's focus on the most rewarding aspect - celebrating growth and healing.

Recognizing Milestones:

As you travel this transformative path, you must recognize and celebrate milestones - moments of growth, change, and healing. These building blocks of your journey deserve acknowledgment.

Create a list of big and small milestones achieved so far. Reflect on how each contributed to your overall progress. This reinforces the value of your journey.

Expressing Gratitude:

Gratitude is a powerful practice that deepens appreciation for the journey. Take time daily to express gratitude for positive changes in your life, no matter how subtle.

Maintain a gratitude journal to record joyful moments, experiences, and people you're thankful for. Gratitude shifts focus from what's lacking to what's abundant.

Cultivating Self-Compassion:

Transformation can be challenging, and setbacks are natural. Self-compassion is essential during these times. Treat yourself with the kindness you'd offer a close friend facing similar struggles.

Acknowledge that setbacks don't negate your progress. They are opportunities for learning and growth. Practice self-compassion by reminding yourself that you're doing your best and that growth is ongoing.

Connecting with Others:

Sharing your journey with supportive and understanding people can be deeply gratifying. Connect with friends, family, or support groups who celebrate your progress and offer encouragement.

When you share achievements with others, it reinforces commitment to personal growth. You may also inspire those around you to embark on their transformational journeys.

Reflection and Integration:

Reflect on your transformation journey - how beliefs, thoughts, and behaviors have evolved. Explore how your subconscious mind has adapted to support intentions.

Integration means incorporating changes into daily life. Consider how to maintain and build upon your progress. What practices and habits will ensure lasting change?

Setting New Intentions:

As you celebrate growth, consider setting new intentions for your ongoing journey - building upon progress or exploring different areas of development.

New intentions keep your journey dynamic, evolving, and purposeful. They provide direction, motivating you to continue exploring your subconscious mind.

Practicing Mindfulness:

Mindfulness enhances appreciation for the present moment. By staying mindful, you can fully savor the richness of your journey - growth, insights, relationships, and experiences.

Practice meditation, deep breathing, mindful walking, and other exercises to ground yourself in the here and now. This allows you to extract more significant meaning and fulfillment from each moment.

Embracing the Journey's Unpredictability:

Finally, embrace the unpredictability of the journey. Your path may take unexpected yet valuable turns - presenting new challenges and opportunities. Rather than resisting these twists, view them as experiences contributing to your growth.

Remember that healing and transformation are continuous processes, not fixed destinations. Embrace the journey as an adventure where each step leads to greater self-discovery and intentional living.

As you celebrate growth and healing, the journey holds immense value. It represents your resilience, courage, and commitment to personal transformation. With each milestone, expression of gratitude, and act of self-compassion, you deepen your subconscious connection and continue blossoming into your highest potential.

"To share your light with others is to reflect the radiance that resides within."

Chapter 11

Sharing Your Journey and Inspiring Others

Welcome back to our exploration of the Restoration Model. We've traversed principles, practices, strategies, challenges, and celebrations. Now, let's consider the profound impact you can have by sharing your journey and inspiring others.

The Power of Sharing:

Sharing your transformational journey is powerful - benefiting you and others. It allows you to reflect on experiences, gain insights, and reinforce your growth. Simultaneously, it inspires and imparts hope to those on similar paths.

You create connection and relatability by opening up about challenges, setbacks, and triumphs. Others may see themselves in your story, finding encouragement and motivation.

Authentic Storytelling:

Authenticity is vital when sharing your journey. Honestly, discuss struggles, vulnerabilities, and successes. Relatable, human storytelling resonates most profoundly.

Share specific techniques, tools, and practices instrumental in your journey. Be transparent about what worked and what didn't. Your authenticity will inspire others to seek growth and healing.

Inspiring Hope and Possibility:

Your journey can ignite hope and possibility in others by demonstrating that positive change is within reach. Witnessing your transformation and growth sparks the belief that they, too, can achieve self-improvement.

Remember, your story need not portray mastery or perfection. Sharing its ongoing, imperfect nature can be even more inspirational, showing that growth is a continuous process.

Offering Support and Guidance:

As you share your journey, some may seek your support and guidance. Be open to listening, providing resources, or recommending professionals to assist their journey.

Sharing your experiences creates community, connecting those facing similar challenges so they can support one another. You become an invaluable resource for those starting their path.

Leading by Example:

Your journey is a powerful example of what's possible with a commitment to growth and healing. Leading by example means aligning your life with your intentions and principles - being the change you want to see.

Demonstrate the principles of intentional living, self-compassion, and resilience in your daily actions. By embodying these, you inspire others to integrate them into their lives.

Creating a Ripple Effect:

Sharing your journey creates ripples of inspiration beyond immediate connections. Those you inspire may motivate others, spreading positive change on a broader scale.

Each person you empower touches more lives, building a network of transformation that extends far through your initial sharing.

Balancing Boundaries:

While sharing your journey is powerful, healthy boundaries are essential. Be selective about details and with whom you share. Prioritize your emotional safety and well-being.

Also, recognize that not everyone may be receptive. Respect others' choices and boundaries, not pushing them to share or change unless they're ready.

Inspiring Your Continued Growth:

Finally, sharing your journey can be a source of motivation for your own continued growth. Knowing your experiences and insights positively impact others fuels commitment to intentional living and development.

As you continue to inspire others, you reinforce dedication to the Restoration Model's principles within your own life. Your story becomes a testament to the transformative power of the subconscious mind and the potential for healing and intentional living within every life.

You contribute to a collective journey of empowerment, healing, and inspiration by sharing your story. You become a beacon of hope, showing others they can embark on transformation paths and create lives filled with intention, purpose, and fulfillment.

"The journey of self-discovery is the pathway to wisdom."

Chapter 12

Sustaining Your Transformation

Welcome back to our exploration of the Restoration Model. We've journeyed through principles, practices, challenges, celebrations, and sharing your story. Let's focus on sustaining the transformation you've worked hard to achieve.

The Nature of Ongoing Transformation:

Transformation is not a one-time event - it's continuous. As your subconscious evolves, your commitment must also be dynamic. New challenges and growth opportunities will arise.

Sustaining transformation means embracing change as integral to your journey. Life and your experiences, beliefs, and perceptions are ever-changing.

Continual Self-Reflection:

Regular self-reflection remains central to sustaining change. Assess the alignment of beliefs, thoughts, and behaviors with your intentions.

Journaling, meditation, and mindfulness aid ongoing self-assessment. By maintaining self-awareness, you can identify deviations from your path and make necessary adjustments.

Integration of New Beliefs:

As beliefs and thought patterns shift, it's essential to integrate changes into daily life, ensuring complete alignment of your subconscious and conscious minds.

Revisit and reinforce positive affirmations and visualization practices. These tools are not just for initial change but for continually strengthening desired beliefs and outcomes.

Staying Resilient:

Life inevitably presents challenges testing resilience. Draw upon cultivated skills and practices in these moments.

Remember the principles of self-compassion, intentional living, and personal empowerment. Use them as your foundation for bouncing back and moving forward with grace and determination.

Maintaining Supportive Relationships:

Relationships nurtured on your journey can provide vital ongoing support and encouragement. Continue to prioritize healthy connections and communication with loved ones.

Share your experiences and challenges with trusted friends or a therapist. Allow their support to bolster your commitment to intentional living and healing.

Adapting to Change:

Your life circumstances and priorities will evolve. Be open to adapting intentions and goals to align with these changes.

Flexibility is invaluable in sustaining transformation. Adjust strategies and practices as needed to accommodate new phases of your life.

Cultivating Patience:

Sustaining transformation requires patience and accepting the natural ebb and flow of progress. Understand that setbacks may occur along the way.

When facing challenges, maintain a compassionate perspective. Use these moments for learning and growth rather than viewing them as failures.

Embracing Ongoing Learning:

Commit to lifelong learning and personal development. Continue exploring new techniques, practices, and resources aligned with intentional living.

Attend workshops, read books, and seek out mentors. The more you learn, the more tools you need to sustain transformation.

Celebrating Milestones Along the Way:

As with your initial transformation, continue acknowledging and celebrating milestones and achievements along your sustained journey. These deserve recognition.

Use gratitude practices to maintain positivity and fulfillment as you continue your path.

Embracing the Adventure:

Finally, sustain transformation by embracing the adventure of intentional living. Approach each day with curiosity, openness, and willingness to explore your subconscious depths.

View your journey as an exciting lifelong exploration of growth and healing. Stay committed to the Restoration Model's principles; knowing this path leads to self-discovery and mindful living.

By sustaining transformation, you enhance your life and contribute to a world where intentional living and emotional healing are valued. Your journey becomes an inspiration, proving change is possible, and growth is a lifelong endeavor.

"Cultivate your inner garden, and your life will blossom."

Chapter 13

Cultivating an Abundant Life

Welcome back to our exploration of the Restoration Model. We've covered principles, practices, strategies, celebrations, and sustainability. Now, let's delve into the art of cultivating an abundant life.

Understanding Abundance:

Abundance is more than material wealth. It encompasses a sense of fullness, richness, and contentment in all aspects of life. Abundance is a mindset and way of being accessible to all, regardless of circumstances.

The Abundance Mindset:

Cultivating an abundance mindset starts with shifting perspective from scarcity and lack to seeing opportunities, possibilities, and the richness surrounding you.

Practice gratitude daily by acknowledging present abundance - loves, health, nature's beauty, and growth opportunities. This magnifies what's already abundant.

Intentional Living and Abundance:

Abundance is intricately linked to intentional living. Living purposefully and aligning actions with values naturally invites abundance.

Identify core values and intentions. Consider what brings joy and your aspirations. Intentional living guides choices in ways that create abundance.

Cultivating Relationships:

Healthy, supportive relationships are vital for an abundant life, providing emotional richness and belonging. Nurture connections with loved ones and the community.

Practice empathy, listening, and open communication. Offer kindness and support, and you'll experience abundant love in return.

Financial Well-Being and Abundance:

While financial wealth alone doesn't determine abundance, it contributes to a secure, fulfilling life. Develop healthy financial habits aligned with your values and goals.

Budgeting, saving, and wise investing can provide financial abundance. But true abundance also means using resources to support well-being and positive contributions.

Embracing Creativity and Innovation:

Abundance often arises from creativity and innovation - exploring ideas, projects, and ventures aligned with passions and interests.

Creativity leads to abundance through artistic expression or problem-solving innovations that improve life for yourself and others.

Mindful Living:

Mindfulness deepens your experience of abundance in everyday life. Be fully present to savor the beauty and richness around you.

Use mindfulness to appreciate simple pleasures - warm tea, a sunset, and quiet reflection. The more you appreciate the present, the more abundant life becomes.

Continuous Learning and Growth:

An abundant life prioritizes continuous learning and growth. Stay curious and open to new experiences, knowledge, and skills.

Make time for self-improvement and pursuing passions. Expanding your horizons reveals the abundance of wisdom and fulfillment lifelong learning offers.

Contributing to Others:

Contributing to others' well-being is a profound source of abundance. Acts of kindness, service, and giving back create purpose and fulfillment.

Engage in generosity, volunteerism, and mentorship. By improving others' lives, you experience abundant meaning and human connection.

Living in Alignment with Values:

To cultivate abundance, ensure alignment of actions and choices with core values. When you live authentically, you feel a deep sense of abundance.

Regularly assess your life priorities and actions to reflect what matters most. Adjust and maintain this alignment.

Gratitude and Abundance:

Gratitude is integral for an abundant life. Daily express your gratitude daily for the abundance you've created and the opportunities ahead.

Consider a gratitude journal to record fulfilling moments and experiences. Gratitude magnifies life's richness.

Celebrating Abundance:

Remember to celebrate your abundance - achievements, milestones, and moments of contentment. Mark your journey and ongoing subconscious transformation.

Abundance is a continuous journey, not a destination. You create a life overflowing with richness, purpose, and fulfillment by nurturing an abundance mindset, intentional living, relationships, creativity, and gratitude.

Your abundant journey demonstrates the Restoration Model's principles. It's a life where your subconscious mind supports your intentions to live with purpose, joy, and prosperity.

"When you change how you look at things, the things you look at change."

Chapter 14

The Ever-Unfolding Journey

Welcome back to our exploration of the Restoration Model. We've covered principles, practices, strategies, celebrations, sustainability, and cultivating an abundant life. Now, let's reflect on the ever-unfolding journey of personal growth and healing.

Embracing the Dynamic Nature of Growth:

Personal growth and healing are not fixed destinations but dynamic, lifelong processes. Life and our experiences, beliefs, and perceptions are ever-changing.

Embrace the idea that growth is a lifelong journey - each day presents new opportunities for self-discovery and transformation. As you navigate this journey, you'll encounter challenges, inspiration, and profound insights.

The Wisdom of Adaptation:

Just as your subconscious adapts to support intentions, you must adapt to life's evolving landscape. Be open to change and learn from experiences.

Adaptation means learning from successes and setbacks, adjusting your course, and integrating new insights into your belief system. This process of continual adaptation allows closer alignment with values and intentions.

Staying Present:

The beauty of the ever-unfolding journey lies in its richness and depth. To fully appreciate it, practice staying present in each moment.

Mindfulness and presence allow you to extract meaning and fulfillment from experiences, relationships, and insights unfolding along the way. Grounding yourself in the present moment allows you to savor the journey.

Reflecting on Your Progress:

Regular reflection is a valuable tool on the ever-unfolding journey. Reflect on growth, achievements, and evolving beliefs and intentions.

Consider keeping a journal to document insights, challenges, and milestones. Reflecting on your progress reinforces commitment to intentional living and development.

Seeking Inspiration:

Stay inspired and committed to learning throughout your journey. Seek new sources of inspiration through books, courses, mentors, and experiences.

Approach each day with curiosity and a thirst for knowledge. The more you engage with the world, the richer your journey becomes.

Nurturing Resilience:

Resilience remains an asset on the ever-unfolding journey. Challenges will test resolve, but resilience allows you to recover and move forward.

Cultivate resilience through self-compassion, a positive mindset, and drawing strength from your support system. Embrace setbacks as opportunities for growth and learning.

Honoring Your Authentic Self:

Throughout the journey, honor your authentic self - your uniqueness, values, and passions. Authenticity guides you toward a life aligned with your most authentic self.

As you honor your authentic self, your intentions become more precise, and your actions resonate with greater meaning and purpose.

Supporting Others:

Consider how you can support others on their growth journeys, sharing wisdom, encouragement, and inspiration. Your willingness to uplift others creates ripples of positive transformation and connection.

Celebrating the Journey:

Finally, celebrate the journey - every moment of self-discovery and intentional living. Reflect on the profound transformation undergone and the beauty of the unfolding journey. Celebrate your courage, resilience, and commitment to lifelong growth.

The eternal nature of the subconscious mind continues supporting your intentions as you both evolve. Your understanding of the subconscious, through the Restoration Model, remains a lifelong tool for intentional living and personal development.

The journey brings continuous opportunities for learning, discovery, transformation, and fulfillment. Embrace it with curiosity, presence, compassion, and celebration.

"Liberating your subconscious and choosing to create the reality you choose is the greatest opportunity to stand in your power and strength."

Conclusion

Embracing the Subconscious Journey to Intentional Living

As we conclude our exploration of the Restoration Model, I want to express gratitude for joining me on this transformative journey.

Throughout this book, we've delved deep into the intricate workings of the subconscious mind, the principles of intentional living, and the immense potential for personal growth and healing. It has been an honor to guide you on this path of self-discovery and empowerment.

In this closing chapter, we'll reflect on key takeaways and distill the essence of the Restoration Model for Emotional Healing. We'll explore how harnessing the power of your subconscious mind can lead to intentional living, emotional healing, and a life abundant in purpose, joy, and prosperity.

Key Takeaways:

The Subconscious Mind: We began by unveiling the profound influence of the subconscious mind over thoughts, emotions, and behaviors. This "silent partner" continually shapes our experiences, developing through significant figures like parents and teachers early in life.

The Subconscious Functions: We explored its multifaceted roles - from storing memories to regulating emotions, making decisions, and learning skills. It became clear that the subconscious guides thoughts and behaviors, choices, relationships, and overall well-being.

Diverse Perspectives: Our journey encompassed distinct perspectives on the subconscious mind across psychology, neuroscience, philosophy, and religion. Each discipline contributed unique insights into its significance and transformative potential.

Primal Motivations: We uncovered the fundamental drivers of human behavior - the pursuit of pleasure and mitigation of fear. These primal motivations underline many choices and actions operating subconsciously. Understanding them empowers more intentional living.

Our Natural State: We explored our natural state, characterized by equilibrium, safety, and functionality. Parental programming, painful experiences, and individual factors shape this state. Recognizing these influences allows deeper self-understanding.

Analyzing the Subconscious: To gain insight into subconscious beliefs, thoughts, and emotions, we learned to conduct comprehensive analyses - examining all aspects of an individual's life and psyche. This profound understanding laid the foundation for transformation.

Methods for Change: We explored diverse methods and practices for cognitive, emotional, and behavioral change, including core belief restructuring, affirmations, visualization, CBT, hypnotherapy, NLP, meditation, and more. These tools empower reshaping the subconscious mind in alignment with conscious intentions.

The Restoration Model: We delved into the Restoration Model for Emotional Healing and its core principles - living presently, intentionally, creatively, powerfully, and in loving relationships with self-understanding. This framework facilitates deep emotional healing and personal growth.

Self-understanding and Empowerment: We discovered that self-understanding is the cornerstone for growth and healing. By comprehensively understanding our core wounds, beliefs, skills, and patterns, we gain the power to create empowering new belief structures and take control of our lives.

Sharing Your Journey: We learned how sharing our transformational journey can profoundly inspire and empower others, creating a ripple effect of positive change. Authentic storytelling provides hope, wisdom, and motivation to those seeking their paths to healing and growth.

Sustaining Transformation: Sustaining transformation demands ongoing self-reflection, integrating changes, resilience, supportive relationships, adapting to change, and lifelong learning and growth. It's a continuous commitment to aligning beliefs, thoughts, and actions with your highest intentions.

Cultivating an Abundant Life: We explored abundantly cultivating a life filled with purpose, joy, meaning, and fulfillment through adopting an abundance mindset, intentional living, nurturing relationships, embracing creativity, mindfulness, learning, and contribution.

The Ever-Unfolding Journey: Our journey concluded with reflecting on the dynamic, lifelong nature of personal growth and healing. This ever-unfolding path demands adaptability, resilience, presence, and celebrating each moment of discovery, transformation, and intentional living.

As you embark on your journey of intentional living and emotional healing, remember the path is not linear but dynamically unfolding. It holds immense potential for continuous growth and transformation. Each moment, challenge, and insight contribute to the richness of your life's tapestry.

May your journey be one of self-discovery, empowerment, and deep fulfillment. May you navigate the landscape of your subconscious mind with grace, resilience, and unwavering intention. May you inspire and uplift others on their paths, co-creating a world where intentional living and emotional healing are cherished.

Thank you for allowing me to guide you on this transformative adventure. Your commitment to growth and healing is a testament to the human spirit's limitless potential. Embrace your subconscious power, live intentionally, and make your life a masterpiece of mindful creation.

"When I learned to master my subconscious beliefs, I could step out of my trauma and into my courage."

Chapter Summaries

Chapter 1:

- Introduces the influential yet hidden power of the subconscious mind.
- Explores the subconscious mind's role in shaping thoughts, emotions, behaviors, choices, relationships, and well-being.
- Discusses perspectives on the subconscious from psychology, neuroscience, philosophy, and religion.

Chapter 2:

- Uncovers the two core drivers of human behavior - pursuing pleasure and mitigating fear.
- Examines how these primal motivations interact and influence the subconscious mind.
- Emphasizes understanding these forces to gain control and intentionality.

Chapter 3:

- Introduces the concept of our natural state - equilibrium, safety, and functionality.
- Explores influences like parental programming, trauma, and physiology in shaping this state.
- Emphasizes self-understanding to achieve a balanced, safe, and functional existence.

Chapter 4:
- Discusses the invisible threads shaping our subconscious - personal history, family indoctrination, and life experiences.
- Highlights how these intertwined forces form the lens through which we perceive the world.
- Encourages examining these threads for self-awareness and growth.

Chapter 5:
- Delves into analyzing the subconscious mind through its hidden layers - behaviors, beliefs, defense mechanisms, etc.
- Explains how comprehensive analysis provides insights into driving thoughts, emotions, and behaviors.
- Set the stage for transformation based on profound understanding.

Chapter 6:
- Explores methods and techniques for transforming the subconscious mind - from CBT to meditation.
- Introduces the Restoration Model for integrating these tools to facilitate emotional healing.
- Emphasizes harnessing subconscious power to create an intentional, purpose-driven life.

Chapter 7:
- Details the core principles of the Restoration Model - mindful presence, intentionality, creativity, empowerment, and loving relationships.
- Highlights self-understanding as the critical foundation for personal growth and healing.
- Focuses on interrupting unhelpful patterns and taking purposeful control of one's life.

Chapter 8:
- Provides practical strategies for implementing the Restoration Model - mindfulness, journaling, affirmations, visualization, and more.
- Offers techniques and exercises to activate the principles of the model in daily life.
- Empowers emotional healing and personal growth through practical application.

Chapter 9:
- Addresses common challenges faced during subconscious transformation - resistance, frustration, self-doubt, and more.
- Offers compassionate perspective and strategies for navigating these obstacles.
- Encourages patience, resilience, and commitment to intentions.

Chapter 10:
- Highlights celebrating growth, insights, and healing during the transformation journey.
- Suggests practices like tracking milestones, cultivating gratitude, and sharing with supportive relationships.
- Focuses on deepening subconscious connection and actualizing one's potential.

Chapter 11:
- Explores the profound impact of sharing one's journey to inspire and empower others.
- Discusses relating authentically, offering guidance, leading by example, and creating ripple effects.
- Reinforces one's dedication to growth by motivating others.

Chapter 12:
- Examines continuously sustaining transformation through ongoing practices - reflection, learning, adaptability, and celebration.
- Emphasizes flexibility, patience, and commitment as crucial for lifelong growth and aligned living.
- Encourages embracing the journey's dynamically unfolding nature.

Chapter 13:
- Delves into cultivating a rich, purposeful, and abundant life.
- Details adopting an abundance mindset and intentionally nurturing well-being, creativity, connections, and growth.
- Emphasizes alignment with values and celebrating the manifestation journey.

Chapter 14:
- Contemplates the ever-unfolding nature of personal growth and healing.
- Discusses adaptability, resilience, mindfulness, authenticity, and supporting others.
- Focuses on honoring each moment of the journey with curiosity and celebration.

"The answers you seek are hidden within your subconscious mind, waiting for you to uncover them."

Journaling Guide

Journaling is a powerful tool for self-reflection, personal growth, and emotional well-being. By putting your thoughts, feelings, and experiences on paper, you can gain clarity, reduce stress, and track your progress over time. This comprehensive journaling guide provides prompts across various areas of life to help you explore and enhance your self-awareness and overall well-being.

Self-Discovery:

1. **Self-Reflection:** Take a moment to contemplate who you are at your core. What are your values, beliefs, and aspirations? How have they evolved over the years?

   _____
   _____
   _____
   _____

2. **Strengths and Weaknesses:** Identify your strengths and weaknesses. How can you leverage your strengths to achieve your goals? How can you improve your weaknesses?

   _____
   _____
   _____
   _____

3. **Life Purpose:** Reflect on your life's purpose and what gives your life meaning. What are your passions and long-term goals? How can you align your actions with your purpose?

   _____
   _____
   _____
   _____

Emotions and Feelings:

1. **Emotional Check-In:** Describe your current emotional state. What emotions are you feeling right now, and what might have triggered them?

   _____
   _____
   _____
   _____

2. **Emotional Challenges:** Explore any recurring emotional challenges you face. How do you typically respond to these challenges, and how can you develop healthier coping mechanisms?

   _____
   _____
   _____
   _____

3. **Gratitude:** List three things you're grateful for today. Reflect on why these things bring you joy and contribute to your well-being.

   _____
   _____
   _____
   _____

Relationships:

1. **Self-Relationship:** How do you perceive and treat yourself? Are there areas where you can be more self-compassionate and nurturing?

   _____
   _____
   _____
   _____

2. **Family Dynamics:** Reflect on your relationships with family members. What positive aspects can you nurture, and are any conflicts needing addressing or resolving?

   _____
   _____
   _____
   _____

3. **Friendships and Social Connections:** Explore your friendships and social interactions. How do these relationships impact your life, and are there any changes you'd like to make in this area?

   _____
   _____
   _____
   _____

Goals and Intentions:

1. **Short-Term Goals:** List three short-term goals you want to accomplish next month. What steps can you take to work toward these goals?

   _____
   _____

_____
_____
_____
_____

2. **Long-Term Goals:** Consider your long-term aspirations. What are your primary life goals, and how can you break them into actionable steps?

_____
_____
_____
_____
_____

3. **Barriers and Challenges:** Identify any barriers or challenges hindering your progress toward your goals. How can you overcome or navigate these obstacles?

_____
_____
_____
_____
_____

Health and Well-Being:

1. **Physical Health:** Assess your physical health and well-being. Are there any habits or lifestyle changes you'd like to implement to improve your overall health?

_____
_____
_____
_____

2. **Mental Health:** Reflect on your mental well-being. How do you manage stress, anxiety, or other mental health challenges? Are there self-care practices you find particularly beneficial?

   _____
   _____
   _____
   _____

3. **Self-Care:** Describe your self-care routine. What activities or practices help you relax, recharge, and prioritize self-care?

   _____
   _____
   _____
   _____

Personal Growth:

1. **Learning and Development:** Consider your intellectual growth. What new skills, knowledge, or hobbies would you like to pursue or explore?

   _____
   _____
   _____
   _____

2. **Overcoming Challenges:** Recall a recent challenge you faced. How did you manage it, and what did you learn from the experience?

   _____
   _____
   _____
   _____

3. **Role Models:** Reflect on individuals you admire or consider role models. What qualities or characteristics do they possess that you'd like to cultivate in yourself?

_____
_____
_____
_____

Daily Reflection:

1. **Today's Achievements:** List three accomplishments or positive actions from your day. Celebrate your achievements, no matter how small they may seem.

_____
_____
_____
_____

2. **Challenges and Learnings:** Describe any challenges you encountered today and the lessons you learned from them. How can these experiences contribute to your growth?

_____
_____
_____
_____

3. **Tomorrow's Intentions:** Set intentions for the next day. What are your priorities, goals, or actions you'd like to take to make the most of the upcoming day?

_____
_____
_____
_____

Creativity and Inspiration:

1. **Creative Expression:** Explore your creative side. What creative outlets or projects bring you joy and fulfillment? How can you incorporate more creativity into your life?

   _____
   _____
   _____
   _____

2. **Sources of Inspiration:** Identify people, places, or things that inspire you. What about these sources of inspiration resonates with you, and how can you draw more inspiration from them?

   _____
   _____
   _____
   _____

3. **Ideas and Innovations:** Brainstorm innovative ideas or solutions to your current problem. Challenge yourself to think outside the box and explore new possibilities.

   _____
   _____
   _____
   _____

Gratitude and Positivity:

1. **Daily Gratitude:** Reflect on the positive aspects of your day. What moments, people, or experiences are you thankful for today?

   _____
   _____

_____
_____
_____

2. **Positive Affirmations:** Write down positive affirmations that empower you. Repeat these affirmations to boost your self-confidence and motivation.

_____
_____
_____
_____
_____

3. **Acts of Kindness:** Describe an act of kindness you performed today or witnessed in others. How did it make you feel, and how can you continue to spread kindness in the world?

_____
_____
_____
_____

Reflection on Past Entries:

1. **Progress Check:** Review your journal entries from the past month or year. What patterns, changes, or growth do you notice in your thoughts and feelings?

_____
_____
_____
_____

2. **Challenges Overcome:** Identify challenges or obstacles you've faced and how you've overcome them. What strategies were effective, and how can you apply them to future challenges?

   _____
   _____
   _____
   _____

3. **Moments of Joy:** Revisit entries that capture moments of pure joy and happiness. How can you create more of these moments in your life?

   _____
   _____
   _____
   _____

"The subconscious is like a vast library of memories and emotions. Explore it, and you'll find the keys to your personal growth."
— Trey Malicoat.

Prompts for Exploring Your Subconscious Mind

As a complement to the comprehensive journaling guide provided earlier, these additional prompts are designed to deepen your journey of self-discovery and subconscious exploration. Use them to better understand your beliefs, emotions, and your subconscious's powerful role in your life. Each section below corresponds to a specific aspect of your subconscious journey.

Section 1: Exploring Subconscious Beliefs

1. **Core Beliefs Examination:** Revisit your core beliefs about yourself, the world, and your capabilities. Select one belief that feels particularly influential in your life. Reflect on where this belief originated and how it manifests in your thoughts and actions today.
   Example: "I believe I'm not good enough because of past failures. This belief came from childhood when I was criticized for not performing well in school."

2. **Beliefs Impacting Relationships:** Consider how subconscious beliefs influence your interactions with others. Identify a specific belief that affects your relationships or communication style. Describe a recent situation where this belief played a role and its consequences.

Example: "My belief that I'm not worthy of love leads me to push people away. In a recent argument with my partner, I withdrew emotionally, creating distance between us."

3. **Beliefs and Decision-Making:** Explore how subconscious beliefs shape your decisions. Choose a recent decision and analyze it, considering your core beliefs. How did these beliefs influence your choice, and what insights can you draw from this analysis?
   Example: "I decided to turn down a job opportunity because of my belief that I'll fail in a high-pressure role. This belief made me miss out on a potentially fulfilling career move."

Section 2: Emotions and Subconscious Insights

1. **Emotional Patterns Deconstruction:** Revisit the recurring emotional patterns you've identified. Select one emotion that tends to surface regularly and explore it further. What triggers this emotion, and how does it connect to your subconscious beliefs or past experiences?
   Example: "I often experience anxiety in social situations. This emotion is triggered by my belief that I'm socially inept due to past embarrassing incidents."

2. **Subconscious Clues in Dreams:** Reflect on any recent dreams you've recorded. Choose one dream and dissect its symbolism and emotions. What do you think your subconscious is trying to convey through this dream, and how might it relate to your waking life?
   Example: "In my dream about falling, I felt vulnerable and out of control. It reflects my fear of losing control in my waking life."

3. **Emotions as Subconscious Messengers:** Emotions often carry messages from your subconscious. Please consider an emotion you're experiencing and consider its message. What

might your subconscious try to communicate, and how can you respond to this message?

Example: "I'm feeling a deep sense of sadness today. I think my subconscious is telling me to address unresolved grief from my past."

Section 3: Relationships and Subconscious Impact

1. **Relationship with Self Reflection:** Return to your self-relationship exploration. Choose a self-critical thought or belief you've identified. How has this belief influenced your self-esteem and choices? What steps can you take to foster a more compassionate self-relationship?
   Example: "My self-criticism has led to low self-esteem and self-doubt. To improve my self-relationship, I'll practice self-compassion and challenge these critical thoughts."

2. **Ancestral Beliefs Exploration:** Delve deeper into the influence of ancestral beliefs on your life. Identify a specific belief or pattern inherited from your family. How has this belief impacted your decisions or relationships? Are there ways to redefine this belief for your benefit?
   Example: "My family's belief in financial scarcity has influenced my money management and caused stress. I can redefine this belief by learning about financial abundance and adopting healthier money habits."

3. **Subconscious Filters in Relationships:** Recall a recent interaction with someone significant. Reflect on how your subconscious beliefs and past experiences shaped your perception of that person and influenced your behavior. How can you navigate these filters to improve your relationships?
   Example: "I felt criticized by my supervisor during our meeting, which triggered memories of my critical parent. To improve this

relationship, I need to separate past experiences from the present and communicate openly."

Section 4: Goals, Intentions, and the Subconscious Navigator

1. **Goal Alignment with Subconscious Beliefs:** Revisit a goal you've been striving to achieve. Examine the alignment between your goal and your subconscious beliefs. How can you adjust your beliefs or actions to support your goal better?
   Example: "I want to start a business, but my belief that I'm not entrepreneurial holds me back. To align with my goal, I'll work on building confidence and seeking mentorship."

2. **Visualizing Empowering Success:** Practice visualizing your goal's achievement again. Dive deeper into the emotional and sensory aspects of this visualization. How does it make you feel, and what actions can you take to manifest this vision?
   Example: "When I visualize running a successful business, I feel excited and proud. To manifest this, I'll create a business plan and seek advice from successful entrepreneurs."

3. **Positive Affirmations in Action:** Implement your affirmations for positive change. Share a recent experience where you challenged a negative belief with a positive affirmation. What were the results, and how can you continue this practice?
   Example: "I used my affirmation 'I am capable' before a challenging presentation. It boosted my confidence, and I received positive feedback. I'll continue using affirmations in similar situations."

Section 5: Well-Being and Subconscious Harmony

1. **Mind-Body Connection Exploration:** Reflect on the connection between your subconscious beliefs and physical well-being. Identify a belief impacting your health or self-care. How can you transform this belief to promote better well-being?

Example: "My belief that I'll never lose weight has led to unhealthy eating habits. To improve my health, I'll work on believing in my ability to make healthier choices."

2. **Mindfulness for Subconscious Awareness:** Revisit your mindfulness journey. Share how mindfulness practices have heightened your awareness of subconscious thoughts and emotions. What mindfulness techniques have been particularly effective for you?
   Example: "Mindfulness meditation has made me more aware of my self-critical thoughts and allowed me to observe them without judgment. It has helped me become more present in my daily life."

3. **Self-Care Aligned with Desires:** Analyze your self-care routine again. Are there additional practices that resonate with your subconscious desires for nurturance and self-compassion? How can you incorporate these practices into your daily life?
   Example: "I realize that spending time in nature aligns with my need for serenity and connection. I'll schedule regular nature walks to enhance my well-being."

Section 6: Personal Growth and Subconscious Evolution

1. **Growth and Subconscious Support:** Reflect on your recent personal growth journey. How have your subconscious beliefs either supported or hindered this growth? Share any pivotal moments where your beliefs shifted positively.
   Example: "My belief in my resilience supported me in overcoming a major setback. It gave me the strength to persevere and grow."

2. **Overcoming Subconscious Hurdles:** Describe a recent challenge or obstacle you encountered. Share your strategies to

overcome it, informed by your understanding of your subconscious. What did you learn from this experience?

Example: "I faced my fear of public speaking by using positive self-talk and visualization. It was challenging but ultimately empowering."

3. **Intuition as a Guide:** Recount an intuitive moment that guided you toward personal growth or an important decision. How did your subconscious contribute to this intuition? How can you further trust your inner guidance?

    Example: "My intuition led me to explore a new career path, which turned out to be a fulfilling choice. I've learned to trust my inner wisdom more."

Section 7: Daily Reflection and Subconscious Navigation

1. **Daily Subconscious Check-In:** Continue your practice of beginning each journaling session with a quick subconscious check-in. How have your subconscious thoughts and emotions evolved since you started this journaling journey?

    Example: "Today, I feel a sense of clarity and purpose in my subconscious. I'm more aware of my self-criticism and actively changing it."

2. **Eureka Moments Abound:** Share any additional moments of sudden insight or clarity that have arisen throughout your daily life. How do these moments correlate with your deepening understanding of your subconscious?

    Example: "While gardening, I suddenly realized how my fear of failure had prevented me from pursuing my passion. This insight aligns with my journaling discoveries."

3. **Acknowledging Subconscious Progress:** Celebrate your ongoing strides in understanding and harnessing your subconscious. How have your thought patterns and behaviors

shifted since you began this journey? What further changes do you aspire to make?

Example: "I've noticed a significant reduction in self-criticism and improved self-esteem. I aim to continue fostering self-compassion and trust in my inner wisdom."

By engaging with these supplemental prompts alongside the comprehensive journaling guide, you'll explore your subconscious mind deeply, fostering personal growth and liberation from limiting beliefs. Your journal will become a trusted companion on this transformative journey of self-discovery and empowerment.

REFERENCES

Caruso, G. D. (2012). Free will and consciousness: A determinist account of the illusion of free will. Lexington Books.

Hartmann, E. (2011). The nature and functions of dreaming. Oxford University Press.

Hassin, R. R., Bargh, J. A., Engell, A. D., & McCulloch, K. C. (2009). Implicit working memory. Consciousness and Cognition, 18(3), 665-678.

Immordino-Yang, M. H. (2016). Emotion, sociality, and the brain's default mode network: Insights for educational practice and policy. Policy Insights from the Behavioral and Brain Sciences, 3(2), 211-219.

Immordino-Yang, M. H., & Damasio, A. (2007). We feel, therefore we learn: The relevance of affective and social neuroscience to education. Mind, brain, and education, 1(1), 3-10.

LeDoux, J. E., & Hofmann, S. G. (2018). The subjective experience of emotion: a fearful view. Current opinion in behavioral sciences, 19, 67-72.

Levine, J. (2015). Unconsciousness and responsibility. In The Oxford Handbook of Moral Psychology.

Malinowski, P., & Lim, H. J. (2015). Mindfulness meditation and the unconscious: a new perspective. Frontiers in Psychology, 6, 1723.

Newberg, A., Alavi, A., Baime, M., Pourdehnad, M., Santanna, J., & d'Aquili, E. (2003). The measurement of regional cerebral blood flow during the complex cognitive task of meditation: a preliminary SPECT study. Psychiatry Research, 106(2), 113-122.

Peres, J. F., Simão, L. M., & Nasello, A. G. (2007). Spirituality, religiousness, and psychotherapy. Archives of Clinical Psychiatry, 34, 82-93.

Westen, D. (1998). The scientific legacy of Sigmund Freud: Toward a psychodynamically informed psychological science. Psychological Bulletin, 124(3), 333–371.

Williams, L. M. (2006). An integrative neuroscience model of "significance" processing. Journal of Integrative Neuroscience, 5(1), 1-47.

INDEX

Abundance mindset: A perspective focused on the fullness, richness, and contentment in life.

Adaptability: The ability to adjust to new conditions and challenges.

Affirmations: Short, positive statements that are repeated to reprogram subconscious beliefs.

Ancestral beliefs: Values, perspectives, or patterns inherited from previous generations in a family.

Attachment styles: Patterns of relating in close relationships that are shaped early in life.

Authenticity: Living and expressing yourself congruently with your actual values and essence.

Awareness: Conscious knowledge and perception of your thoughts, feelings, and experiences.

Behaviors: Actions, reactions, and habits demonstrated by an individual.

Beliefs: Ideas and perspectives that shape how we perceive reality.

CBT (cognitive behavioral therapy): A therapeutic approach focused on identifying and changing negative thought patterns.

Celebrating growth: Acknowledging and appreciating victories, insights, and positive changes during your journey.

Challenges: Difficulties and obstacles encountered on the path of change and growth.

Change: The process of transitioning from one state or condition to another.

Communication: The exchange of information between individuals through speaking, writing, signals, or behaviors.

Conscious mind: The aspect of mind comprising thoughts and perceptions we know.

Contribution to others: Acts of generosity, service, and adding value to other people's lives.

Controlling behaviors: Reactions and habits enacted to create a sense of predictability and order.

Core belief restructuring: Thoroughly examining and replacing ingrained beliefs that shape our perceptions.

Creativity: The ability to generate original ideas, solutions, and innovations using imagination.

Decision making: The process of selecting a course of action from multiple possibilities.

Defense mechanisms: Tactics the ego uses to protect against anxiety, unpleasant emotions, or psychological pain.

Desires: Subjective feelings of longing, wishing, or wanting specific outcomes or experiences.

Developmental stages: Phases of growth and maturation through life based on emotional, social, and cognitive changes.

Dreams: Sequences of images, storylines, emotions, and symbols experienced during sleep.

Driving forces: Fundamental motivations and needs influencing behavior such as pursuing pleasure and mitigating fear.

Emotions: Subjective feelings and physiological reactions that strongly influence mood and behaviors.

Empowerment: Gaining power, confidence, and control over your choices and life circumstances.

Equilibrium: A state of harmony between opposing forces and internal balance.

Experiences: Events and situations that shape development, perspectives, and beliefs.

Exposure therapy: A technique that helps individuals overcome fears by gradually and safely exposing them to an object or situation that causes anxiety.

Family dynamics: Relational patterns, communication styles, and collective behaviors within a family system.

Fear: An emotion triggered as a response to perceived danger or threat.

Flexibility: The ability and willingness to adapt or change course in response to circumstances.

Functionality: Effectiveness, competency, and ability to successfully manage life's tasks and challenges.

Goals: Desired results, outcomes, accomplishments, or achievements individuals work toward.

Gratitude: Appreciation and thankfulness for people, experiences, and blessings in life.

Growth: Progress in developing skills, maturity, emotional intelligence, and positive change over time.

Healing: The process of recovering from distress, trauma, or dysfunction to reach a state of wellness.

Health: Physical, mental, social, and emotional well-being.

History: Past events, experiences, and developments that shape an individual or group.

Hypnotherapy: A technique using guided relaxation and focused concentration to access the subconscious mind.

Impatience: Difficulty waiting calmly for desired results and wanting immediate gratification.

Influences: People, experiences, or factors that shape perspectives, beliefs, and behaviors.

Innovation: Introducing new methods, ideas, technologies, or solutions that improve processes or experiences.

Insight: Moments of sudden clarity, realization, and profound understanding.

Intentions: Desired aims, objectives, and commitment to carrying out actions and plans.

Intuition: An instinctive knowing or insight arising from the subconscious rather than logical reasoning.

Journaling: Documenting thoughts, feelings, experiences, goals, and growth through writing.

Joy: A feeling of happiness, pleasure, and gladness.

Kindness: Being friendly, generous, and considerate in treating others.

Learning: The acquisition of new knowledge, behaviors, skills, or ways of thinking through experience and study.

Limiting beliefs: Perspectives or assumptions that narrow possibilities, constrain potential, and hold you back.

Living intentionally: Making conscious choices aligned with values, purpose, and goals rather than living reactively.

Love: A profound feeling of deep affection, care, connection, and fondness.

Maladaptive patterns: Habits, behaviors, or thought processes that are counterproductive or harmful.

Memories: Recollections of past experiences and acquired information stored by the mind.

Mentors: Trusted advisors who share knowledge, experience, and wisdom to support growth and development.

Milestones: Significant events, achievements, or turning points marking progress on a journey.

Mindfulness: A mental state of present-moment awareness, focused attention, and nonjudgmental observation.

Mindset: An established set of attitudes and beliefs that shape your outlook.

Mistakes: Errors in action, thinking, or judgment caused by ignorance or impulsiveness.

Motivations: Internal needs, desires, and incentives that propel action and behavior.

Natural state: The baseline mode of functioning we gravitate toward based on inherent tendencies and equilibrium.

Neuro-linguistic programming (NLP): A methodology using language patterns and perceptions to influence thoughts and behaviors positively.

Obstacles: Barriers, impediments, or hurdles that hinder progress.

Openness: Willingness to consider new perspectives, ideas, information, opinions, or experiences with an open mind.

Overcoming challenges: Successfully managing and moving past difficulties and setbacks.

Parental programming: Core beliefs and patterns conditioned by parents and caregivers early in childhood.

Patience: The capacity to wait calmly, tolerate frustrations, and accept life's delays and challenges.

Patterns: Consistent themes, tendencies, dynamics, and recipes for thinking and behaving that repeat over time.

Perseverance: Continued commitment and determination despite difficulties, obstacles, and delays in achieving goals.

Personal empowerment: Taking ownership and control of your choices, path, and future rather than giving power away.

Perspectives: Viewpoints, angles of approaching something, and subjective interpretations of events.

Pleasure: Feelings of happiness, enjoyment, joy, comfort, or satisfaction derived from experiences.

Practices: Activities, routines, processes, or techniques regularly followed to develop skills.

Presence: Focusing awareness and attention intentionally on the here and now with an open, accepting attitude.

Programming: Established thought, emotion, and behavior patterns learned through repeated experiences.

Progress: Forward movement and evidence of growth, learning, and development.

Psychopathology: Deviations, dysfunctions, and disturbances in emotions, behaviors, perceptions, or social functioning indicating mental illness.

Purpose: A meaningful aim, intention, or calling that motivates and guides your choices and actions.

Reciprocity: Mutual giving and receiving of support, effort, benefits, and well wishes between parties in a relationship.

Reflection: Conscious consideration, contemplation, and rumination to deepen learning and self-awareness.

Relationship patterns: Habitual social interactions, communication styles, and individual dynamics.

Relapse: Reverting to unhealthy thought patterns or behaviors after a period of positive change.

Religion: Organized systems of practices, beliefs, rituals, and symbols to facilitate closeness to the sacred or transcendent.

Resilience: Capacity to recover, adapt, and bounce back after adversity, setbacks, hardship, or trauma.

Resistance: Inner defense against and avoidance of discomfort associated with healing, challenge, or change.

Restoration Model: A holistic framework to understand and positively reshape the subconscious mind.

Rewards: Positive results and benefits that follow effort, progress, or achievement.

Ripple effect: The continuing influence and impact of an action or event that spreads beyond the initial point.

Safety: Freedom from harm, danger, or anxiety from perceived threats or risks.

Self-analysis: Objective observation, examination, and evaluation of your thoughts, feelings, and behaviors.

Self-care: Activities and practices that replenish, nourish, and revitalize your mental, emotional, and physical health.

Self-compassion: Treating yourself with kindness, care, and understanding in the face of failures, setbacks, or inadequacies.

Self-confidence: Assured trust in your abilities, qualities, and judgment to successfully manage situations.

Self-criticism: Harsh judgment of your perceived flaws, failures, and inadequacies.

Self-discovery: Gaining deeper understanding, knowledge, and awareness of your essence, beliefs, desires, and patterns.

Self-doubt: Lack of confidence and belief in your abilities, preventing you from moving forward.

Self-empowerment: See personal empowerment.

Self-esteem: How you evaluate your self-worth, competence, and capabilities.

Self-kindness: Treating yourself with gentleness, patience, and understanding.

Self-knowledge: Extensive understanding of your character, emotions, desires, capabilities, and behaviors.

Self-motivation: Inner drive and incentive to accomplish goals and persist despite challenges and setbacks.

Self-relationship: Your pattern of beliefs, feelings, expectations, and treatment toward yourself.

Self-trust: Reliance on your core self, intuition, and inner wisdom to guide you.

Setbacks: Reversals, delays, or temporary failures impeding progress.

Sharing your journey: Openly conveying your growth process, insights, and experiences to inspire others.

Short-term goals: Desired accomplishments and outcomes intended to be achieved soon.

Skills: Developed abilities and learned expertise, allowing the execution of tasks.

Spirituality: Belief in, connection to, and pursuit of a dimension beyond the self, communion with the sacred.

Staying present: Maintaining awareness of the here and now with acceptance and nonjudgment.

Strengths: Natural capacities, talents, qualities, and capabilities you excel at or possess.

Stress management: Techniques, practices, and lifestyle choices to manage and reduce stress.

Struggles: Difficulty, distress, hardship, suffering, and anguish experienced in overcoming challenges.

Subconscious mind: The part of the mind containing thoughts, feelings, urges, and memories outside conscious awareness.

Support system: A network of people who provide practical and emotional support.

Sustainability: Consistently maintaining behaviors, practices, and positive changes over time.

Teachers: Instructors facilitating learning and development through knowledge, skills, and guidance.

Therapy: Treatment and interventions, often guided by a professional, focused on healing and growth.

Thought patterns: Habitual cognitive responses, reasoning styles, assumptions, and associations.

Time management: Effectively organize and budgeting time to achieve goals and complete tasks.

Transformation: A marked change in nature, function, or condition from one state into another.

Transitions: Changing processes between life stages, circumstances, or identities requiring adjustment.

Trauma: Complicated, distressing, or disturbing experiences causing psychological injury or damage.

True self: Your essence is characterized by inherent qualities and values vs. conditioned personality.

Trust: Confident reliance on the integrity, strength, and reliability of a person or process.

Uncertainty: The state of being unsure, undefined, unknown, or unable to predict the future.

Values: Principles, standards, and qualities considered worthwhile, meaningful, or morally desirable.

Victories: Successes achieved through determined effort, discipline, or courage.

Visualization: A mental imagery technique using vivid sights, sounds, and feelings to imagine desired outcomes.

Vulnerability: Willingness to share innermost thoughts and feelings openly, despite risks or uncertainties.

Weaknesses: Deficiencies, limitations, or areas needing improvement that require focused effort to strengthen.

Well-being: Positive physical, mental, social, and emotional health and quality of life.

Wisdom: Deep understanding and ability to discern inner truth gained through life experience.

ABOUT THE AUTHOR

Trey Malicoat is a writer, counselor, educator, and thought leader in emotional health. Trey has worked in mental health and education since 1996 and is the creator of the Restoration Model for Emotional Healing and the founder of the Restoration Academy.

Trey has written several educational pieces, classes, and presentations on mental health, trauma, LGBTQIA issues, human sexuality, grief, and mindfulness.

Trey has taught at Western Oregon University, The University of Oregon, Oregon State University, The University of Denver, and several community colleges.

Trey, his partner, and their dog Flash live in Denver, Colorado. They enjoy great food, interesting conversations, travel, and laughing a lot!

www.ingramcontent.com/pod-product-compliance
Lightning Source LLC
Chambersburg PA
CBHW061453040426
42450CB00007B/1341